Country Music's Most Embarrassing Moments

James L. Dickerson

Cumberland House
Nashville, Tennessee

Published by Cumberland House Publishing, Inc.
431 Harding Industrial Drive, Nashville, Tennessee 37211

Cover : Beverly A. Cruthirds, Cruthirds Design

Library of Congress Cataloging-In-Publication Data

Dickerson, James.
    Country music's most embarrassing moments / James L. Dickerson.
    Includes index.
    ISBN 1-888952-33-4
    1. Country musicians--Anecdotes.   I. Title.
  ML65.D53 1996
  781.642'092'2--dc21   96-46449
                                                              CIP
                                                              MN

Printed in the United States of America
1 2 3 4 5 6 7 — 02 01 00 99 98 97 96

To my son,
Jonathan

Contents

✷ Introduction ✷

EMBARRASSING MOMENTS ARE the sticky stuff that cement memories. Stuck between every great, heroic moment in our lives are those pesky little intrusions that remind us of our vulnerabilities. We've all had them. We're all glad to see them in others. They are God's way of letting us know all is well in the universe.

Sometimes it is hard to believe celebrities ever have embarrassing moments. On the surface, their lives often seem perfect. In truth, celebrities are exposed to more embarrassing moments in one year than the average person experiences in a lifetime. When they share those moments, it has an unusual effect—it makes them seem more real to us. It makes us like them even better.

In my 20-year career as a journalist, I have interviewed my share of celebrities. So many, in fact, that it could well be that if you consider yourself a celebrity—and you have not been interviewed by me—you may want to re-examine your celebrity credentials. You may be a celebrity poser and not an actual celebrity. Over the years I have been eye-witness to celebrity goofs galore. And I have been the victim of my own missteps. Such as the time I was interviewing a noted radio personality and mentioned another radio personality who had been convicted of taking payola. I expressed a low opinion of the deejay for breaking the law, then during a long, awkward pause suddenly remembered my interviewee had himself been convicted of taking payola. Talk about dead air space.

By far my most embarrassing moment with a celebrity occurred during my first interview as a journalist. I was a student at the University of Mississippi. Although my major was in English and psychology, I took a full load of journalism classes that semester. The year was 1967. The song that everyone was talking about was Bobbie Gentry's "Ode to Billie Joe." In August it hit the No. 1 slot on the *Billboard* charts and stayed there for four weeks. Bobbie Gentry was the biggest star in the world in the fall of 1967. She was particularly big in her home state of Mississippi.

I was in class one day when my professor announced that Bobbie Gentry was returning to Mississippi to attend a homecoming ceremony in her hometown of Houston. A murmur went through the class. That was big news. After class I asked the professor if I could attend the homecoming and write a story for the student magazine *Mississippi*. His first response was to laugh. Another professor had already tried to schedule an interview with the singer and had been told she would not do any interviews during her visit. If a professor could not get an interview, he sug-

gested, what chance would
a student have? The pro-
fessor looked puzzled.
"Have you ever written a
story?" he asked. I shook
my head. "You won't get
an interview," he warned,
"but why don't you go for
the experience. At least,
you'll get to see the national press corps at work."

Bobbie Gentry in 1967

Before heading out for
Houston, I wrote out a list
of about 20 questions. I wanted to be prepared in case I
did get an interview. At the end of the list, I tossed in sort
of a joke question, one I thought might be good for a
laugh. Maybe I had never done an interview, but I had
seen plenty of movies and, as everyone knows, a good
movie always ends with a laugh. At least they did in 1967.

For Houston, Bobbie Gentry's homecoming was an
event of unprecedented importance. Banners flourished,
high school bands marched, official and unofficial recep-
tions welcomed with open arms that town's first — and
only — recording star. It was Christmas and the Fourth of
July wrapped into one. Without much trouble I located
Miss Gentry at a reception at a local motel (the only motel

in town I think). She was surrounded by well dressed admirers. Everyone wanted to shake her hand. I saw her talking intimately to a man who had that blond, surfer-guy look that branded him an out-of-towner. I figured she was with him. Turned out she was. He was her producer. After some maneuvering, I pulled him aside and told him I was there to interview Miss Gentry. Not a chance, he told me, smirking.

"*Time, Newsweek*, they all sent reporters and we've had to say no to everyone," he said, barely able to contain his glee at turning me down. "Sorry. She just wants to enjoy her visit."

Later that day the town gave a luncheon in her honor at the school cafeteria. The tables were lined up in a U-shaped configuration. Of course, Miss Gentry and the town dignitaries were seated at the place of honor at the bottom of the U. I was seated at the top of the U, along with about 100 other reporters. The only difference I could see between the national reporters and the local reporters was that the national reporters had more pens in their shirt pockets. I was impressed. I had only one pen in my shirt pocket. But I was learning.

I listened to the speeches and then ate lunch, acutely aware that I would have to do something drastic if I had any chance of getting an interview with Bobbie Gentry. I took a deep breath. Then I rose to my feet and walked around the table into the open part of the U. As a hush fell over the room, I strode confidently up to where Miss Gentry was seated. You could have heard a pin drop. I put my hands on the table and leaned over into her startled face.

"I'm a student at Ole Miss and if I don't get an interview with you I'll be in big trouble," I whispered. Bobbie Gentry smiled. The mayor, who was seated next to her, did not smile. He looked around for a police officer. Her producer, who was seated on the other side of her, grimaced. He glared at me with that special type of contempt I have since learned is possessed only by record producers. "Please," I said.

Bobbie smiled. There was a twinkle in her eye. After a moment, she nodded, yes.

"You can't," the producer said, annoyed. "We don't have time."

Bobbie reached out to shake my hand. "I have one more reception at the motel," she said. "Meet me there and I'll talk to you then."

With that, I whirled around and faced my competitors in the press corps. Everyone stared at me as though I had done something unmentionable, which of course I had. I was so pleased with myself I goose-stepped all the way back to my seat.

The reception seemed to last an eternity. I sent several messages in to Bobbie to remind her that we were going to talk. Each time she got my message she looked up and

waved. Finally, her producer walked over and—not looking particularly happy—told me it was time to do the
interview. He said the motel had offered a room for the
interview.

As Bobbie, her producer and I walked across the
courtyard to the motel room, I realized we would not be
alone in the room. With Bobbie was a friend from Los
Angeles, a striking blonde who could have passed for a
leggy, supermodel, and the local deejay, a nerdy guy with
a plastic pen holder in his shirt pocket. Joining that group
were six Mississippi Highway Patrol officers, all armed
with revolvers.

We entered the room and Bobbie sat in a chair next to
the bed. I sat on the edge of the bed next to Bobbie. Her
friend lay across the bed and curled up around me. The
highway patrol officers lined up along the wall. The deejay and the producer stood a short distance away.

I cannot imagine a more intimidating situation in
which to do an interview. For a novice, such as myself, it
was terrifying. If I thought I would have a few quiet
moments alone with Bobbie I was sadly mistaken. Bobbie
lighted a cigarette and a stone cold silence fell over the
room. "Hush," someone said to a fidgety highway patrol
officer. He stood at attention.

I was absolutely terrified.

Bobbie was wearing a mini skirt and her legs were crossed only inches away from my notepad. The photos taken of her at that time did not do her justice. In person, she was one of the most striking women I have ever seen. She had been a dancer in Las Vegas and that experience clearly was reflected in her long, well-defined legs. She radiated sexuality, something I did not expect. Behind me, her friend's body pressed against me as she made herself comfortable on the bed.

Bobbie looked at me and smiled. "So, what's your first question," she asked.

I panicked. I fumbled with my notepad, but I couldn't find my list of questions. Every page I turned to was blank. The only question I could remember was the last one I had written down, the joke question. I was desperate.

"So what's your favorite fruit?" I asked lamely.

Bobbie looked shocked. Everyone in the room looked shocked, even the state troopers.

After a moment, Bobbie recovered. She pursed her lips into a devilish smile. "If you think I'm going to say bananas, you're crazy," she said, laughing. Everyone laughed at Bobbie's joke. Then they laughed some more — at me.

"I think you can do better than that," Bobbie said.

I did, but the embarrassment of that moment still makes my ears tingle.

ENJOY THE EMBARRASSING moments shared with you in this book by country music's elite. Laugh with them and at them. Appreciate their honesty. In compiling this book I discovered a thing or two I did not know when I began. I learned which artists are too insecure to discuss their embarrassing moments (look at who is in the book and who is not and figure it out for yourself) and I learned whose ego would not allow them to admit moments of embarrassment. If your favorite country music stars are not in this book, it may be because they were too busy (fat chance)—or it may be because they live lives of wimpish desperation and have not yet learned to laugh at themselves.

At the count of three, laugh at them anyway.

— James Dickerson

Country Music's
Most Embarrassing
Moments

Chet Atkins

★ CHET ATKINS ★

SOME 20 OR 25 years ago, I was a guest with the Portland, Maine Symphony. After playing my opening number, and a couple of other tunes on the electric guitar, I put the guitar on the stand and picked up my acoustic nylon-string classic guitar.

As I did this, I felt a draft below my belt. Upon inspection, I noticed that my fly was unzipped. At the same time a young man in the first row was holding up a large sign telling me that my fly was open.

I, of course, corrected the situation, and after the show I autographed his sign. It should have been embarrassing, but no way. I just laughed it off. That has happened only one other time. But it's no problem. It is only a problem if one forgets to unzip.

CHET ATKINS IS one of the true giants of country music. A world class guitarist, his distinct style of playing has influenced scores of country, rock and jazz musicians. He has released too many albums to list in this space (well over a hundred), but some of his best include "Chet

Atkins Picks the Best," which won a Grammy in 1967, "Snowbird," a 1971 Grammy winner, "Me and Jerry," a duet with Jerry Reed that won a Grammy in 1970, and "Chester and Lester," a collaboration with Les Paul that won them a Grammy in 1976.

Aside from his musical ability, Atkins is distinctive for the business and moral leadership he has given to the industry. In 1972 he was honored by the National Council of Christians and Jews, which gave him its Humanitarian Award. He is one of the very few performers in the business to survive five decades of success without the slightest hint of scandal. In 1973 he was elected to the Country Music Hall of Fame.

Atkins got his first big break in 1946, when he first appeared on the Grand Ole Opry. In the late 1940s he performed with the legendary Carter Family. By 1949, as his records made a impact on the country music scene, he was hired as a staff session player for RCA Records. By 1957 he was working as a producer for the label and by 1968 he was put in charge of the entire label. I once asked him about that promotion. "I was kind of ashamed of that because I wanted to be known as a guitarist and I know, too, that they give you titles like that in lieu of money," he said, displaying his wry humor. "So beware when they want to make you vice president. The paycheck would be better (if they didn't)."

In recent years, Atkins has taken off his record executive hat, but he continues to make records—he did a album project with Suzy Bogguss in 1994. When he's not in the studio, he can usually be found on the golf course.

Garth Brooks
with wife, Sandy

★ GARTH BROOKS ★

"I f Tomorrow Never Comes" was written for three of the best friends I ever had in my life. Two of them were Jim Kelly and Heidi Miller. Jim died in a plane crash in 1982 and Heidi died in a car crash in 1984. The third best friend in my life is my wife, Sandy.

The song was written for those people. It was also written for anyone else who would like to say that if tomorrow never comes, "I want to tell you how much I love you." It's a song I wrote with Kent Blazey and it means the world to me. Now I feel that I have told Jim and Heidi that I loved them, when in life I never did. When Sandy, first heard it she cried. She cried a lot.

The first time I ever played it was on a show called New Country on the Nashville Network. I got past the first chorus and it starts talking about the friends that I've lost. Jim and Heidi's face kept hitting me in the face. All of a sudden I looked down and saw my wife sitting out there in the audience. The hair on the back of my neck stood up and my eyes started watering. I tried to get them to retape it, but they wouldn't. I was pretty embarrassed by that. I haven't had that problem since because I just try to think of something else because that song means an awful lot to me.

GARTH BROOKS' DEBUT album had just been released by Capitol Records. His publicist, Pam Lewis, called me and asked if I would have him as a guest on my syndicated radio program, "Pulsebeat—Voice of the Heartland." I hadn't heard his album, but I had featured other country artists represented by Pam and I agreed to have him on the show based on her promise that he was a pretty good singer. Mark Carter, head of publicity at Capitol at that time, sent over his album and I listened to it and pulled several songs to use on the show.

When Brooks showed up at the studio, we were interviewing someone else at the time and he took a seat in the waiting room and patiently waited his turn. He seemed nervous. Once in the studio, he relaxed and thanked us over and over for having him on the show. I don't know if the interview we did with him that day was his first, but if it wasn't it was probably only his second or third. The excitement clearly showed on his face. He seemed amazed that anyone would want to talk to him about his music. During the interview, he was honest about dreams, trials and tribulations, and his hopes for the future. It was from that interview that the above anecdote was drawn for this book.

I don't think the song mentioned above, "If Tomorrow Never Comes," had been released at the time of the interview, but, of course, it later became one of his most popular—and requested—songs. Interestingly, when the Garth Brooks program was aired, a number of radio station program directors called me to protest. Garth Brooks had no future in country music, they said, and if I sent any more programs their way that contained similar no-talent performers they would cancel their contracts.

In the years that followed that interview, Brooks' label changed its name from Capitol to Liberty and then back again to Capitol, Pam Lewis became his manager (only to part company with him in 1994) and Brooks went on to become the best selling country music artist of all time.

T. Graham Brown

★ T. GRAHAM BROWN ★

WE WERE DOING a show with Ronnie Milsap and Kenny Rogers in Virginia. It was outdoors and drizzling. During sound check Ronnie always paces the stage to be sure that he knows how many steps it is to the edge. Then he'll get up in the middle of his show and walk right up to the brink and not fall into the crowd. It's a great gag and always shocks the audience.

Anyway, during my opening set I was walking backwards and tripped over a floor monitor and fell into the drum set, wiping out microphone stands, cymbals, breaking the big bass drum head wide open, and cutting my hand while trying to break my fall.

Nine thousand people thought it was hilarious. When Milsap came out after me, he did his stage walking bit and told the crowd: "Ain't it funny? I'm blind and can walk on this stage just fine. Brown can see and still busts his behind!"

T GRAHAM BROWN'S DEBUT album, "I Tell It Like It Used To Be," sent tremors along Nashville's Music row when it was released in 1984. Never before had a country singer so blatantly blended honky tonk and blue-eyed soul into one package. His first single, "Drowning in Memories," charted and the follow-up, "I Tell It Like It Used To Be," made the Top 10. The third single, "I Wish That I Could Hurt That Way Again," made the Top 5. He followed those successes up with back-to-back No. 1 singles—"Hell and High Water" and "Don't Go To Strangers."

Brown's second album, "Brilliant Conversational-ist," spawned three more hits: "The Last Resort," "She Couldn't Love Me Anymore" and "Brilliant Conversationalist." A third album, "Come As You Were," continued the tradition with the No. 1 hit, "Darlene."

In 1990 "T" recorded a duet with Tanya Tucker titled "Don't Go Out," a song that brought him a 1991 Country Music Association nomination in the duet category. In 1993 he won a CMA Award in the Vocal Event of the Year Category for his part in the George Jones single, "I Don't Need Your Rocking Chair."

Since the early 1990s he has augmented his music career with excursions into television and film. Actually, his movie experience pre-dates his recording career. While still living in his hometown of Athens, Georgia, he landed bit parts in the Richard Pryor film, "Greased Lightning," and in "The Curse," which John Schneider and David Keith. In 1988 he got a part in "Heartbreak Hotel," playing the role of Elvis Presley's right-hand-man, Jerry Schilling. In the 1990s he continued his television appearances, becoming a regular on TNN's "Music City Tonight," and did a series of high-profile TV commercials for Taco Bell that featured his singing and his acting in the fast-food company's "Run For the Border" campaign.

"T" continues to maintain a busy touring schedule.

Kenny Chesney

★ KENNY CHESNEY ★

My MOST EMBARRASSING moment was when I was in third grade at Luttrell Elementary School in East Tennessee. It was during PE. This girl kissed me on the bleechers and I peed in my pants.

My grandmother worked in the cafeteria and she called my mom and she had to come to the school and everybody knew that I had peed in my pants. When she got there, they called me over the intercom. They said for Kenny Chesney to please come to the office to get his new pair of jeans.

It was so embarrassing to have to get up and walk to the office and get a dry set of underwear and a dry set of jeans. All because of a kiss. Since then I've gotten more used to it (kissing, that is).

KENNY CHESNEY RELEASED his BNA debut album, "All I Need To Know," in 1995. Prior to that he released an album on Capricorn in the early 1990s, becoming one of that label's first country acts. "All I Need To Know" fared well with critics. "From the start of

'Grandpa Told Me So,' which extols the virtues of family wisdom, to the start of 'Bigger the Fool,' which offers the admonition that 'her long legs look like trouble,' you know there is no pretense in Chesney's music," wrote one reviewer. "It's old-time country, no apologies offered."

Chesney came from a musical family (his mother and aunt were regulars on a gospel radio show), but he took a circuitous route on his way to Nashville. First he considered a career as a baseball player, then, while attending East Tennessee State, he got interested in music. He learned to play guitar and tried his hand at songwriting. After graduating in 1990 with a degree in marketing, he moved to Nashville to pursue a career as a songwriter. A string of day jobs later—he parked cars, worked in the mailroom of a record company—he got his first big break and was signed to a publishing contract by Opryland Music.

Chesney worked with other songwriters such as Whitey Shafer and Dean Dillon, then Aaron Tippin asked him to go out on the road with him. Other offers followed and he toured with Confederate Railroad, Trisha Yearwood, Charlie Daniels and Patty Loveless. At about the time Kenny was making a name for himself on the road, Capricorn disbanded its country division. BNA wasted no time in signing Chesney and pairing him with legendary producer Barry Beckett, who cut his studio teeth on r&b sessions in Muscle Shoals, Alabama. That pairing created a real boots and roots album that gave Chesney a sound that could best be described as honky tonk soul.

Mark Chesnutt

★ MARK CHESNUTT ★

I WAS PLAYING BY myself at a real little club in Beaumont, Texas. Nobody ever paid much attention to me at all. Then one day when I was playing, I heard this clap, clap, clap.

I thought, well, finally somebody's listening to me.

I thanked whoever it was and then I found out later it was some guy trying to get catsup out of a bottle. That was embarrassing!

MARK CHESNUTT HAS released four albums since 1990, three of which have been certified platinum. He's had more than a dozen Top 10 singles, including "Brother Jukebox," "Blame It On Texas," "Your Love is a Miracle," "Sure is Monday," and "I Just Wanted to Know," all of which went to No. 1. The Country Music Association gave him its Horizon Award and an award for Vocal Event of the Year for his part in George Jones' "I Don't Need No Rocking Chair."

A native of Beaumont, Texas, he was weaned on country music by his father, who released a couple of singles on an independent Nashville label in the late 1960s. He has said that some of his earliest memories involve going into honky-tonks with his parents to hear the singing and watch the dancing. Perhaps because of that lifelong interest in country music, he has been called a walking jukebox, someone whose knowledge of honky-tonk music covers the spectrum from famous to obscure. Yell out a song title to him and, chances are, he'll sing it on the spot.

After dropping out of high school his sophomore year, and performing "any place that would have me," he got his first break when he was booked at George Jones' theme park, "Jones Country." After opening for Merle Haggard, Hank Williams Jr and Willie Nelson at the park, he attracted the attention of Nashville music executives who happened to hear a song he recorded and released on a regional basis. That song, "Too Cold at Home," recorded for Cherry Records, convinced Mark Wright, head of A&R at Decca, that Mark Chesnutt had a future in the music business. Wright signed him to a record deal, and when his first single, "Too Cold at Home," was released to a national audience it promptly went to No. 2.

Chesnutt quickly followed up the success of his debut album with "Longneck and Short Stories" in 1991 and "Almost Good-bye" in 1993. He released two albums in 1995, "What a Way to Live" and "Wings."

Terri Clark

★ TERRI CLARK ★

I WAS IN THE fifth grade and it was 1978. I can't quite recall the name of the school 'cause I went to five or six different ones before the sixth grade. We moved a lot!

Anyway, we were in Home Room class getting ready for phys. ed. class. We always wore our shorts for phys. ed. underneath our street clothes so we could change quickly right there in class. (Don't ask me why! Whatever happened to locker rooms?)

That particular day my head must have been in the clouds because I proceeded to strip down to my gym shorts right there in the classroom with the other kids, and, to my and everyone else's amazement, I had forgotten to wear them! So, there I stood with my pants down around my ankles in my underwear, in front of my entire fifth grade class.

The teacher looked at me like I had committed a crime and the class erupted in laughter. I'm still embarrassed when I think about it and to this day I'm still pretty modest!

Terri Clark released her self-titled debut album in 1995, eight years after moving to Nashville in search of her dream of becoming a country music star. Her maternal grandparents, Ray and Betty Gauthier, were popular country music stars in Canada. During the 1950s and 1960s the Gauthiers often opened for Little Jimmy Dickens, George Jones and Johnny Cash. Clark's mother, Linda, was a folk singer and performed in coffee houses during her pregnancy with Terri, leading her to believe that her mother's love of music "must have sunken in."

Clark wasn't sure what to expect when she moved to Nashville right out of high school. On her third day in the city, she wandered into a downtown lounge that featured live music. Within 30 minutes the lounge owner offered her a job as a house singer.

To support herself over the next few years, she performed in local clubs, sold boots and waited tables, doing whatever it took to survive. For seven years she worked on her skills as a songwriter and struggled to get a record deal. She got her chance in 1994. She was taken into the Mercury Records office on Music Row for a live audition for the label's president, Luke Lewis. The following day she was offered a contract.

Terri is proud of the fact that she co-wrote 11 of the 12 songs on her first album. "They've got real simple lyrics that everybody can understand," she says. "And I think waiting tables, selling boots and working with so many people has to do with the earthiness of the lyrics. This is real people music."

Confederate Railroad

★ CONFEDERATE RAILROAD ★

TEN YEARS AGO, back before we were Confederate Railroad, we were right in the middle of a show when a federal marshal comes into the club. He walks up to me on stage and flips his badge. He asks for Chris McDaniel, our keyboard player, and I just point over in his direction.

There in front of 800 people he tells Chris he is under arrest for child molestation and the interstate transportation of a minor for illicit purposes and statutory rape. Chris' eyes get about the size of silver dollars. Then he leads Chris out through the middle of the crowd to the front of the building and frisks him where everyone can watch.

Chris was just 18, but he was maintaining fairly well until one of our crew members, a pretty good sized guy, walked outside and said, "What's the damn problem here?" The marshal, who was a huge guy himself, said, "This don't concern you, boy. Git back inside." When he said that, it was so scary sounding, Chris' knees buckled and he hit the floor, moaning, "Oh, God. Oh, God." But it was all a joke we set up on Chris.

It was his first time on the road with us. Some friends of his family, a lady named Johnnie Sue and her 16-year-old daughter, had come down to see Chris in his first show. Since Chris was 18 and the daughter was 16, we got to kidding him. We'd tell him, "We know nothing is going on, but this is Florida and they aren't going to understand you spending so much time together." So we got the marshal—and he was a real federal marshal—to arrest him on stage as a joke.

Poor Chris, he was just a kid. But he got over it—after a while.

— Danny Shirley

CONFEDERATE RAILROAD'S SELF-TITLED debut album produced several hits, including "Trashy Women" and "Queen of Memphis," before going platinum in 1993. That same year they were chosen Best New Vocal Group by the Academy of Country Music. The group's second album, "Notorious," spun out even more hits, including "Redneck Romeo," "Daddy Never Was the Cadillac Kind" and "Elvis & Andy."

Despite the sudden appearance of Confederate Railroad on the charts, there is nothing new and shiny about the 6-member group, which has been playing the nightclub and honky tonk circuit for a decade. The group is composed of: Chattanooga native Danny Shirley, who does the lead vocals; Michael Lamb on guitar; Chris McDaniel on keyboards, bassist Wayne Secrest; drummer Mark DuFresne and pedal steel guitarist Gates Nichols.

Confederate Railroad has an outlaw image that is reflected in their music and in the way individual members dress, which could probably best be described as Southern biker gothic. They get that image honestly. It certainly wasn't designed by consultants in New York. For years, the band went out on the road with "outlaw" acts such as Johnny Paycheck and David Allen Coe, and did shows with southern rockers such as Lynyrd Skynyrd. That experience enabled them to develop an energetic, hard-edged style that has made them a popular attraction on the concert circuit.

"We've been out there so long, with so many influences, we can play to just about any crowd," says Danny. "And we can play the same show for George Jones' people that we play for Lynyrd Skynyrd's people."

Bobbie Cryner

★ BOBBIE CRYNER ★

MY MOST EMBARRASSING moment will be titled, "20 Minutes in My Own Private Hell." (Okay, so that's a slight exaggeration. It was more like 10 minutes.) Having a "love-hate" relationship with restaurants, it would only be appropriate that some of my most embarrassing moments have taken place in them. On what started out to be a beautiful winter night, my manager, Erv Woolsey, was taking me to meet Tony Brown for the first time. [Editor's note: Tony Brown is head of MCA Records.]

Knowing that Tony is an extremely talented, powerful, good-looking, SINGLE man, not to mention a snappy dresser who possibly held my entire future in his hands, I set out to impress him. Assuming we weren't going to meet at "Western Sizzlin,'" I chose to wear a stunning black and leopard jumpsuit for my petite flower of a little body. (Okay, so it was a little small. From the rearview it didn't look much unlike double-knit polyester stretched over 10 pounds of chewed bubble gum. Okay, are you satisfied?)

Anyway, my greatest fear was that I would appear extremely nervous and uncool. Which I was. But I was happy that the dinner was going well. Clear up until my triple "Death by Chocolate," I was making it through relatively unscathed. After five cups of coffee and a lot of professional nods and comments such as "Yes, that's a great idea!" I excused myself to the powder room. Once inside the stall, I proceeded to disrobe. (I HAD to! It was a jumpsuit.) Anyway, after I went, much to my chagrin, I discovered my entire sleeve had been in the toilet. I was gone a total of 20 minutes washing and attempting to dry my clothes. By now, just the time alone that I was gone was embarrassing enough in itself.

I walked out to join everyone, tripped on the carpet and promptly sat myself down at the table. The remainder of the evening was spent trying to hide my arm. Behind the chair, under the table, etc. The fact that Tony would grab my arm when he was making a point, only added to my embarrassment. I'm sure he wondered why it was wet up to my arm pit, and why I kept pulling it away. Turns out my greatest hope for the evening is that maybe he thought I was just extremely nervous and perspiring profusely as any uncool, wannabe, hope-I-am-impressing-you-person would. I hope so.

WHEN BOBBIE CRYNER exploded on the music scene in 1993—seemingly from nowhere—she was compared to country music legends such as George Jones and Patsy Cline. Her self-titled debut album attracted praise not only from country music publications, but from *Rolling Stone* and *Entertainment Weekly*. *The Hollywood Reporter*, not known for gushing reviews of country releases, said: "With an alluring honey-and-molasses voice, Bobbie Cryner is an outstanding find in country, not just another new girl singer, but a w-o-m-a-n."

The critics were so enthusiastic about Cryner's debut album, she was quickly snatched up to be the opening act for the George Strait tour. Although Cryner's passionate, stone-country vocal style evokes memories of pre-Garth Brooks generations, there is nothing traditional about her views on the music industry. "A lot of women are taking the forefront, but I think we need a lot more," she says. " I think we need more women in the business and in production...so we have a bigger say in what we record and what we don't record."

Despite the critical success of her first album, and Nashville music community's acceptance of her as a rising star, the outspoken redhead quickly found herself at odds with her record label. In 1995 she left Epic Records and signed with MCA Records. That introductory meeting with label head Tony Brown is described in the above embarrassing moment.

Lacy J. Dalton

★ LACY J. DALTON ★

ONCE, IN THE early 1970s, shortly after the death of my first husband, and long before my first record deal, I was traveling in the West with my 3-year-old son, Adam, and a girlfriend. We had had some unforeseen and major car trouble which totally cleaned out our piggy bank. Since we were in Reno, Nevada, at the time, and since, fortunately I had brought along a guitar, I was able to go door-to-door, cowboy bar to casino, looking for some instant work.

At one small casino, the owner took pity on me and agreed to an audition. (I had explained to him, of course, that I was utterly marvelous.) To this day I don't know if it was his compassion or my talent that got us that hot meal and fifty dollars, but I am still grateful.

Anyway, when it came time to sing, I gathered up my floor length, blue skirt and walked to the stage with as much dignity as could be mustered and explained to the audience the circumstances of my being there. I also explained that having told the proprietor how "simply fabulous" I was that I hoped they would show mercy and clap loudly no matter what.

I then proceeded to seat myself grandly upon the only stool available (a 3-legged drum stool) whereupon the flimsy little thing collapsed loudly beneath me, sending me head-over-tea-cups with the aforementioned skirt somewhere in close proximity with my ears.

Needless to say, the audience went wild with laughter, which did not stop for what seemed like forever. Each time the crowd would find the strength to stop howling, I would start a song and then collapse into laughter myself.

Needless to say, I have never "broken the ice" so successfully with a new audience since, and I'll wager that casino owner never ever had a more entertaining lounge act for fifty dollars and a couple of hot meals.

B Y THE TIME Lacy J. Dalton found success in 1980, she had put in more than a decade of hard work as a struggling singer/songwriter, often supporting herself on minimum wage earnings as a short-order cook or charwoman.

"I still feel like a working class person," she said in 1986 on the eve of the release of a new album, "Highway Diner." "I've never made so much money in this business that I've ever been more than a working class person."

Dalton began her career as a rock singer. But after 15 years of the psychedelic rock scene, she decided it wasn't for her. In 1978 she recorded an album that contained a number of country songs, many of which she wrote herself. She distributed the album in northern California. As fate would have it, a Nashville record executive heard the album and offered her a recording contract. The following year the Academy of Country Music chose her as its Top New Female Vocalist.

Since 1980 she has recorded 14 albums, three of which were "greatest hits" compilations. Her hit singles include "Crazy Blue Eyes," "16th Avenue," "Dream Baby," "Black Coffee" and "Hillbilly Girl with the Blues."

Whether because of her rock background or her unique vocal style, which has a gritty, smoky quality to it, she has carved a niche for herself in country music. People magazine once called her "country's Bonnie Raitt." That's pretty close to the mark.

Although Dalton hasn't released any new material since the early 1990s, she currently plays about 120 dates a year and is a frequent performer at Las Vegas and Reno.

Holly Dunn

★ HOLLY DUNN ★

O N A RECENT visit to a radio station, I was greeted quite enthusiastically by a very friendly man who seemed to be waiting for me in the lobby. After spending several minutes being shown around the station, he headed me towards a studio to do an interview.

Just outside the studio door, we ran into the disc jockey with whom I was originally scheduled to do my on-air interview. He said he had been looking for me. As this DJ and I stood there chatting, a funny look came over the face of the man who had shown me around the station as he slowly realized that perhaps he had mistaken me for someone else.

I'll never forget the look of total horror and embarrassment when it dawned on him that I was Holly Dunn, the singer, and not the lady from the Red Cross there to talk about the local blood drive!

S INCE 1986 HOLLY Dunn has released eight albums. She has scored a number of No. 1 hits, including "Love Someone Like Me," "Only When I Love," "Are

You Ever Gonna Love Me" and "You Really Had Me Going." In 1986, the year her first album was released, she was named the Academy of Country Music's Top New Female Vocalist.

The following year she won the Country Music Association's Horizon Award. She has had three Grammy nominations, including one for "A Face in the Crowd," a duet she recorded in 1988 with Michael Martin Murphy. Although she hasn't recorded a lot of duets in her career, one she did with Kenny Rogers, "Maybe," made the Top 20. "Daddy's Hands," the song for which she is probably best known, was not a No. 1 hit but it did make the Top 10.

A native of San Antonio, Texas, Dunn began her career penning songs for artists such as Louise Mandrell, Christy Lane and the Whites. Her first recording contract was with a new label called MTM Records. Unfortunately, the label went out of business after releasing three albums by Dunn—"Holly Dunn (1986)," "Cornerstone (1987)" and "Across the Rio Grande (1988)." Dunn quickly signed with Warner Bros. Records and between 1989 and 1992 she released four albums on that label—"The Blue Rose of Texas," "Heart Full of Love," "Milestones—Greatest Hits" and "Getting It Dunn."

After creative differences lead to a parting of the ways between Dunn and Warner Bros. in 1992, she took a couple of years off from recording to focus on her songwriting. In 1994 she returned to the studio to record an album for River North Records. Titled "Life and Love and All the Stages," the album was released in 1995 and received enthusiastic reviews. Dunn wrote all of the songs on the album but one. "I feel like this album is me finding my way back to the music," she says.

Janie Fricke

★ JANIE FRICKE ★

W E WERE PLAYING for President Reagan at Camp David, Maryland. We walked out on stage and we did our first song and the PA system didn't work. It was like total silence.

We kept singing. We couldn't stop. We were singing at the swimming pool and they were seated across the pool from us. They could see us singing and playing, but, of course, they couldn't hear what we were playing and singing.

That was a pretty bad moment. We were so nervous to be performing before the President. To us, that was the most humiliating thing that could have happened.

J ANIE FRICKE HAS recorded 23 albums since 1978. Her hits include "Don't Worry 'Bout Me Baby," "He's a Heartache" and "Your Heart's Not In It." She has been chosen "Top Country Female Vocalist" or "Female Vocalist of the Year" by Billboard Magazine, Music City News Cover Wards, the Country Music Association, the Academy of Country Music and Cash Box Magazine. A performance with Charlie Rich was nominated for a Grammy in the "Best Duet" category and she was nominated for a Grammy in the "Best Female Performance" category.

While still a student at the University of Indiana, Fricke began her career in Memphis, Tenn., singing advertising jingles for the same company that helped launch the career of Rita Coolidge. After trying her luck in Los Angeles, and not having much success, she moved to Nashville in 1975, where she sang jingles for products such as 7-Up, Coca-Cola, United Airlines and Red Lobster. She quickly made a name for herself as a backup singer, working on sessions with Elvis Presley, Ronnie Milsap and Barbara Mandrell.

Fricke's career as a solo artist was launched by a single line she sang as a backup singer in Johnny Duncan's No. 1 hit, "Stranger." After the line, "Shut out the light and lead me," leaped out of the song, everyone, including recording executives, wanted to know who she was. The man who produced "Stranger," Billy Sherrill, wasted no time in trying to sign her to a recording contract. Interestingly, Fricke was reluctant at first to give up a very successful career as a jingle singer. But Sherrill was persistent. Fricke turned her back on jingles and has never looked back. In 1977 her first solo single, "What're You Doin' Tonight," made the top 20. A string of hits followed in the late 1970s and 1980s. Her most recent album was "Greatest Hits Now & Then," recorded in 1993.

Fricke currently lives in Texas and maintains a busy concert schedule.

Vince Gill

★ VINCE GILL ★

JOE GALANTE AND I were friends before we became business associates. (Editor's note: Joe Galante is head of RCA Records/Nashville.) Our first meeting was in Houston. I was playing guitar in Rosanne Cash's band. Tony Brown, who was head of A&R at RCA at the time, told Joe, "You've got hear this guy, Vince. He needs to be making records."

So he came down to Houston. Obviously we had way too many cocktails after the show. We had to get the paramedics there to revive one of our buddies. That was Joe and I's first meeting, saving a friend's life. The friend had totally abused himself and passed out.

We carried him upstairs in one of the luggage carts at the hotel. He was pretty crazed. The next time we spent any time together, I ended up staying at his house. I started out the door, made about three steps and turned around—"make me a bed, pal; I ain't going nowhere."

VINCE GILL HAS won as many country music awards as anyone in history. He's received five Grammys, including one in 1995 for "When Love Finds You," four Academy of Country Music awards and 13 Country Music Association trophies, including one in 1995 for Entertainer of the Year (his second). That's not bad for an Oklahoma boy whose early success were with the Blue Grass Alliance and then the pop/folk group, Pure Prairie League, whose song, "Let Me Love You Tonight," was a Top 10 hit in 1980.

After several years of performing in college, rock-oriented venues with Pure Prairie League and working as a session player on albums with Bonnie Raitt and Dan Fogelberg, he gravitated to Nashville and decided that country music was where he belonged. RCA released his first album in 1984. His second album, "The Things That Matter," was released in 1985. That was when I first met him. I was in Nashville to do a feature article on four artists I thought had a future in country music. Gill was one of my picks, along with Marty Stuart.

Gill was appalled at the way country music was being watered down by pop music techniques. He felt country music fans wanted the real thing. "People are starting to want those raw edges," he told me then. "They want more humanness back in recording."

During the mid-to late 1980s, Gill's career crept along at a snail's pace. In 1988 I invited him to be a guest on my radio syndication, "Pulsebeat—Voice of the Heartland."

The above anecdote was taken from that interview, which was conducted by my announcer, the beautifully exotic Kim Spangler. What I remember most about that interview is that mid-way through the anecdote, Gill paused to do an aside—asking himself if he should be telling that story—then, in typical Vince Gill fashion, overruled himself and proceeded with the story.

A year or so after the interview, Joe Galante left RCA Nashville to head up the pop division in New York. Tony Brown moved over to MCA Records and so did Gill when his contract with RCA expired. In late 1994 Galante returned to Nashville to head up the country division and, at last glance, Gill and Brown were still churning out monster hits for MCA.

Eddy Raven

★ EDDY RAVEN ★

WE WERE IN Dallas at the state fair grounds in 1987. We were doing a show that the Dallas police were involved in. I think it was the Fraternal Order of Police. There were probably about 10,000 people there that day. I think Dottie West was on the show, but I don't remember who else was there.

They had this barrier in front of the stage and there was this board that went from the stage out to the barrier. I stepped out on the board during a song because a lady had brought some kids and wanted me to shake their hands. I was wearing these Italian pants. They were pretty tight. When you clean them for some reason they say you have to be careful or it will destroy the thread. All of a sudden the board broke. My foot slipped and I straddled the board. I didn't miss a note singing, but when I crawled back up my pants were split all the way down. I didn't have any underwear on that night. Why, I don't know. But I didn't know my pants were split. I kept on singing.

Sonny West, who played with Elvis all those years, came running over. So did all the other guys in the band. Sonny said, "Bubba, your pants are broke! They're split wide open!" Sonny grabbed my coat and put it around me and I finished the song.

It felt a little airy, but I wasn't hurt.

SINCE 1969 EDDY Raven has released 20 albums, including seven greatest hits collections and four Christmas compilations. A string of No. 1 hits such as "I Got Mexico," "Bayou Boys," "Joe Knows How To Live" and "Shine, Shine, Shine" quickly established him in the 1970s as the dominant voice of Cajun country music. But Raven, whose first love was rock 'n' roll, took his music well beyond the confines of the regional sounds of Louisiana that first attracted attention to his music. He developed a high-energy concert style that for more than two decades has made him one of the most sought after live performers in the business. With a unique mix of Cajun, country, rock and blues music, he has forged an identifiable style that has yet to be duplicated.

A prolific songwriter, Raven has written numerous hits for other artists. He penned "Thank God For Kids" for the Oak Ridge Boys, "Good Morning Country Rain" for Jeanne C. Riley and "Back in the Country" for Roy Acuff. He also wrote songs for Roy Orbison, Jerry Reed and Moe Brandy. He has won over 30 ASCAP songwriting awards.

Among the nearly two dozen Top 10 singles recorded by Raven are: "Sooner Or Later," "Operator, Operator," "A Little Bit Crazy," "Sometimes a Lady," "'Til You Cry" and "I Wanna Hear it From You."

Ronna Reeves

★ RONNA REEVES ★

ONE OF MY most embarrassing moments happened in Odessa, Texas, where I was raised. I was working at a rodeo at Dos Omegos. They had asked me to sing the national anthem before the riding started, but, actually, when I got there I forgot they had asked me. Since I really wasn't polished up on the words, I had a friend write them out for me on a piece of paper. All my friends were there. My family was there. I was excited.

I got up on stage and realized I had to kick it off. But none of my musicians were around. I thought, well, I can figure this out. I started the song off and I realized I had started way to high. As I'm going along, I'm reading the words. All of a sudden, all of the words were wrong. I totally panicked. Not only did I not know the words, I was in a key in which I would not be able to hit the big punchline.

That was the first time in my life I ever stopped singing. You can't just make up words to the national anthem. I stopped and everyone starred at me. My face was beet red. I said, "You know, I can't remember the words to this song." I looked out at the audience. They didn't look angry, but they didn't look happy either. I saw my mom looking down at the ground.

Luckily for me there was a guy in the audience who knew the words. He stood up picked it up where I left off and took it on from there. I was ready to crawl under the stage. I had always been told, whatever you do, don't stop. But you can't just make up words to the national anthem.

That was 10 years ago and I did not sing the national anthem again until last year. Let me tell you, I knew that song like the back of my hand. There was no way I would mess it up again.

🎻

RONNA REEVES HAS released four albums since 1991: "Only the Heart," "The More I Learn," "What Comes Naturally" and "After the Dance," her most recent release (1995). In 1994, she accomplished a first for a country music artist. One of her songs, "He's My Weakness," was used as theme music for the ABC day-time drama, "One Life To Live." The song garnered Reeves a nomination for a Daytime Emmy.

Like many other country music artists, Reeves, now 29, got an early start in the music business. She began her career at the age of 9 and by the age of 11 she had her own 3-piece band that was performing in clubs in Texas. By

17, she was opening for George Strait, a job that lead to other opening act offers from Garth Brooks, Randy Travis, The Judds and Ronnie Milsap.

"I didn't have an ordinary childhood," she says. Then she laughs. "I think I've been paying a lot of dues."

"After the Dance" marked Reeves' debut as a songwriter. "It took me three years to finally do that," she says. "Lyrics are very important to me. I have to sing something I can relate to. I want to sing about reality and what people go through as well as the fun songs."

For Reeves that reality is no further away than her own life experiences. "Generally I am pretty upbeat and I do have a lot of energy, but I've also been through a lot in my life. I've gone through a bad divorce, I've had everything I owned stolen. I think I'm a serious person, a strong person who's been through a lot and I want to be perceived that way."

Riders in the Sky

★ RIDERS IN THE SKY ★

I BELIEVE I FORFEITED my Right to Embarrassment 3145 shows ago when I put on a huge hat and a Cac-Tie and became Too Slim. Sure, there are thousands of instances in my so-called career which would mortify a lesser man into catatonia, but to me they just go with the territory. I knew the job was tough when I took it.

One circumstance does stand out, however, in the flood of unplanned pratfalls, hecklers who were funnier than me, and involuntary onstage allergic reactions. It happened the day before we were to open in Las Vegas at the Sahara, our first big Vegas show.

Woody left me by the side of the road in Utah when I got out to pee and buy a *USA Today* and a Creamsickle. He thought I was still in my bunk. I was unshaven, dressed in a dirty T-shirt and cut-offs, and layered with 35 hours of road cheese.

I walked four miles into a tiny town, bought a bus ticket to Sin City, and arrived about midnight. The Las Vegas bus station at midnight is not a dull place. I asked a guy how to get to the Sahara. He looked me up and down and suggested I go three streets over and take the bus and "save the money." I sat behind the driver.

There it was in screaming neon, fifteen foot letters, a show biz dream come true. "Don Rickles with Riders in the Sky." "Hey, that's us! That's my band," I yelled at the driver. "Sure it is, pal," he said. "Sure it is."

— Too Slim

I'VE HAD MORE than a few embarrassing moments in my life, but the one that everyone keeps reminding me about happened a couple of years ago when we were playing John Asquaga's Nugget in Sparks, Nevada.

We were just beginning a two weeks engagement and about the second or third night we were playing to a full house in the 8 o'clock show. That always attracts a big family crowd and the three of us were on stage just doing what we normally do.

We were about halfway through the show and Slim seemed to notice some snickering and giggling in the first few rows. Normally that's pretty normal in a Riders in the Sky show, but not when Ranger Doug is in the middle of one of his codependent, dysfunctional love songs. I was not paying a whole lot of attention, just happily playing my fiddle and having a good time. I should have been paying attention.

Pretty soon the song ended, the applause died down, and instead of some conversation about the next song, I was met with Too Slim's lyrical voice announcing to me and the other 2,000 people in the room, "Woody…your fly is open."

You hear stories about this same thing happening to everyone and it's always a good laugh. It's an even bigger and better laugh when it happens to you!

— Woody Paul

RIDERS IN THE Sky has been delighting audiences with its cowboy humor and romantic ballads for nearly 20 years. The trio, composed of Ranger Doug, Woody Paul and Too Slim, directs its act toward a family audience and its greeting—"A great big Western howdy to all you Buckaroos and Buckarettes out there!"—has become a familiar trademark.

The group's most recent album, "Cowboys in Love," features songs such as "One Has My Name, the Other Has My Heart," which they recorded with Emmylous Harris, and "I'm a Ding Dong From Dumas," which they did with the Western swing group, Asleep At the Wheel.

"'Cowboys in Love' was just a flat-out fun record to make," says bassist Too Slim. "I like to think our playing and singing gets better all the time. That's what keeps us going, that feeling that we keep growing and finding new ways to play the songs and entertain people."

Their weekly radio show, "Riders Radio Theater," is in its fifth season and is broadcast to 170 public and commercial markets across the U.S. In 1995 they hosted four one-hour specials for TNN and released an instructional video on harmony singing. They also have plans for a series of programs for children's videos. Even with all of their radio and television work, they still manage to do about 200 concert dates a year. Most performers would consider that schedule hectic, but not the tried-and-true cowboys of the radio. "We're at a stage in our career where a lot of guys just lie back and cruise," says Ranger Doug. "We go out on stage every night looking for something new to do."

Riders in the Sky has performed regularly on the Grand Ole Opry since the early 1980s.

Johnny Rodriguez

★ JOHNNY RODRIGUEZ ★

I GREW UP IN south Texas. A lot of times in Sabinal, Texas, you run out of things to do. There's just not much to do in a little town like that. One night, my friends and I went out. There were about 18 or 20 of us kids, and most of us were under 18. We decided we wanted to have a barbecue, but we didn't have anything to barbecue, so we went out in the country and stole us some goats.

Some of us had beer. We were out to have a good time. We weren't out to hurt anybody. I didn't even realize at the time that it was a felony to steal goats. We got caught, and I took the rap for the goat stealing and got three to seven years in prison for it.

"So what would you do differently if you had it to do all over again?"

I'd lie about them goats.

J OHNNY RODRIGUEZ RELEASED his first album in 1972. Titled "Introducing Johnny Rodriguez," it shocked him—and his record label—by going to No. 1 on the charts. His follow-up album made it into the Top 10 in

1973, as did the next one, "My Third Album," released in 1974. By that time, he had become one of the hottest new acts in Nashville, earning him a distinction as the first Mexican-American to achieve success as a country artist.

As his popularity increased on radio, he tried his hand at acting, making his debut on the television show, "Adam-12." Encouraged by his reception as an actor, he accepted a role in the movie, "Rio Diablo." During the late 1970s, he followed up his early recording successes with "I Wonder If I Said Goodbye," a No.1 hit in 1977, and "If Practice Makes Perfect."

By the mid-1980s his career had slowed down. I met him 1988, when he told the above goat-rustling story at a Pulsebeat interview. As embarrassing as it was to get caught stealing goats, the incident ultimately lead to his discovery as a recording artist. While he was in jail a Texas Ranger, who had known him as a youth, dropped by one day and asked him to sing for the sheriff and the deputies. After he had impressed the local law authorities with Johnny's talent, the Texas Ranger arranged to get him released on work detail at a tourist attraction, Alamo Village. It was there that he met a promoter who then introduced him to country star, Tom T. Hall, who eventually gave him a job with his band.

Rodriguez still tours and records on a regular basis.

T. G. Sheppard

★ T. G. SHEPPARD ★

ONE OF MY most embarrassing moments was with Clint Eastwood. I was appearing at Lake Tahoe's at Harrah's. People are always doing practical jokes on me. Especially the guys in the crew and in the band. After you've been on the road a couple of weeks, everyone gets a little squirrely. So to pass the time, we do a lot of practical jokes on each other.

I was in the hotel suite one day. It was about noon. The operator calls and says, "I have Clint Eastwood on the phone." I said, "Sure put him through." Then I said, "Hello, who is this?" He says, "This is Clint Eastwood." I said, "Yeah, and I'm Ronald Reagan."

The phone got real quiet.

I said, "Hello." He said, "Yes." Then there was something about the way he spoke and I recognized the voice. I thought, Oh, my God. I said, "Clint, I'm sorry. I thought my boys were pulling a prank." He said, "Aw, I understand." I told him I was a big fan of his and just figured someone was pulling my leg.

Not long after that, I flew to L.A. and we did the duet, "Go Ahead, Make my Day." When I met him, I said, "Clint, how are you?" He said, "I'm fine, Mr. President, how are you?"

T G. SHEPPARD HAS had a remarkable career that spans three decades. Born in Humboldt, Tennessee, he moved to Jackson at the age of 16 to work as a sideman in various country bands. From there, he went to Memphis, where he joined the Travis Womack band as a guitarist and backup vocalist. Before long, he had a recording contract with Atlantic Records. He released several singles using the name Brian Stacy, one of which, "High School Days," made a respectable showing on the charts.

For several years, he gave up performing to work as a record promoter. He worked for Stax Records and RCA Records and eventually started his own promotion company. During that time he became a friend and confidant of Elvis Presley. While helping promote the records of other artists, he came across a song titled "Devil in the Bottle," which he thought was a hit. He tried to get several people to record it, but no one was interested. Finally, he recorded it himself. In February 1975 it became the No. 1 country record in America.

Sheppard followed up the success of that record in 1975 with another No. 1 hit, "Tryin' To Beat the Mornin' Home." Another Top 10 hit followed later that year, "Another Woman." Since then he has had countless hits on the country charts, including "When Can We Do This Again?" "Solitary Man," "Happy Together" and "You Feel Good All Over."

Sheppard opened a performance theater in 1995 at Gatlinburg, Tennessee, where he performs on a regular basis.

The Statler Brothers

★ THE STATLER BROTHERS ★

IT WAS A hot night in Charlotte, N.C. The Statlers were headlining a show at the Charlotte Coliseum. It was a standing-room-only crowd and I remember thinking just before we were announced that everything seemed to be perfect, right down to our new clothes. It was that period of time when we were wearing matching outfits. Tonight they were brand new, tailored, flag-designed white gabardine suits.

We made quite an entrance. The crowd roared. We sang our first song, took a bow and when I bent over, the seat of my brand new, white pants ripped from the belt to the crotch. Now I realized that I had to stay out there on the stage for about an hour and fifteen minutes and I would not be able to hide a rip that big for that long.

So I made a quick decision. I stepped up to the mike, told the 12,000 people what had happened, then bent over and showed them. They must have enjoyed me sharing my embarrassment, because the show was great, the people had a good time and the reviewer didn't mention it. Guess it's kind of a "cool" way to do a show.

— Harold Reid

THE STATLER BROTHERS have described themselves as gospel singers who do country music with a rock 'n' roll band—and that is a fairly accurate description. Of course, as their fans know, the Statler Brothers are not brothers (two of them are) and their name is not Statler. Their real names are Don Reid, Harold Reid, Philip Balsey and Jimmy Fortune, who replaced original member Lew DeWitt in 1982.

Shortly after the group first got together, they were booked to tour with Johnny Cash. They needed a name for the group, but nothing they thought of seemed right. A box of Statler Tissues, a regional brand of paper tissues, was on a nearby table. Someone suggested they become Statlers, and the name stuck.

After touring with Cash for three years, they signed a recording contract with Cash's label Columbia Records. Their first single, "Flowers on the Wall," zoomed to the Top 10 on the country charts and to No. 1 on the pop charts in 1966. The song also won two Grammy awards for the group. Throughout the 1970s the Statler Brothers were one of the most successful groups in country music. Their hits include "Bed of Roses," "Do You Remember These?" and "I'll Go to My Grave Loving You." After four years with Columbia, the group switched to Mercury Records, where they have remained ever since.

For three decades the Statler Brothers have been turning out hit records and winning virtually every award offered. From 1971 through 1980, for example, they were named Top Vocal Group in the Music City News Cover Awards. For seven years in a row they won the Country Music Association's Award for Top Vocal Group. They have recorded 47 albums in their career, and the most recent, a collection of their favorite hits from the 1950s, was released in 1995.

When Cash hosted his own variety show in the late 1960s and early 1970s, the Statlers were a regular feature. In 1981 they played themselves in Burt Reynold's "Smokey and the Bandit 2," which included their song "Charlotte's Web" on the soundtrack. In 1992 they began hosting their weekly, variety show on TNN.

Incredibly, the Statler Brothers have the same enthusiasm for their work they had when they began. During a break in the recording of their last album, "The Statler Brothers Sing the Classics," which features songs such as "Love Me Tender" and Unchained Melody," Don Reid was brimming with excitement. "We have not enjoyed ourselves so much in the studio in 30 years," he said.

Marty Stuart

★ MARTY STUART ★

I WAS OUT ON tour with Sammy Kershaw. We had a great setup. We had a rocket ship on stage and this big teepee that I would duck into for costume changes. Sammy was aggravated because the teepee took up a lot of his stage room. It was aggravating, and I understood that; but we didn't have any choice if we were going to use it.

Well, one night I went in the teepee to change during a fiddle song. There was a squaw sitting there and she had no clothes on. Sammy had paid her to go into the teepee and take her clothes off.

"So, it's your birthday," she said.

"Uh huh." I said, "Would you like a drink of water?"

About that time, she started looking around the teepee, getting nervous. All of a sudden, she started for the door. She was going to run onto the stage with no clothes on.

"No, no, no," I said. "Get your britches on. You can go out the back."

After she left, I looked out the door and saw Sammy and the others standing to the side of the stage, giggling. I went back out on stage and dedicated the next song to Running Bear and left it at that.

MARTY STUART IS only a year shy of turning 40, but he already has 25 years of country music under his belt. That's because as a 12-year-old "boy wonder" guitar picker, his father took him to a bluegrass festival to hear the Lester Flatt and Earl Scruggs band. Stuart made friends with the mandolin player and the following year, at the tender age of 13, he went to Nashville for a visit — and he never left. With his parents' permission, he joined Flatt's band as a picker and toured with the group until Flatt's death in 1978.

For the next several years, Stuart honed his skills as a picker, adding mandolin to his arsenal of musical weapons. In 1980, while producing a memorial album to Flatt, he saw Johnny Cash's name and phone number in an open book in producer's office. He called Cash, introduced himself and asked him to be on the album. Cash did the album, then the next year he returned to be on Stuart's first album, "Busy Bee Cafe," recorded for Sugar Hill, an independent label that specializes in blue grass music.

I first met Marty Stuart in 1985. He had come to Memphis with Cash to play guitar on Cash's songs on the "Class of '55" album, that also featured Jerry Lee Lewis, Carl Perkins and Roy Orbison. Stuart had just signed a recording contract with CBS Records and his head was spinning with ideas for the first album. Unfortunately, it was bad timing for Stuart's raw-nerved, energetic style and when the album was released it was not embraced by the public. Stuart kept going.

"There's a rage inside me," he told me in 1986. "Sometimes it makes me kick over plants. Other times it makes me go on stage and go past my limits."

Stuart's career at CBS Records never met his expectations. It was not until he switched to MCA Records that he found his audience—and it found him. Inducted into the Grand Ole Opry and elected to the board of the Country Music Foundation, he shucked his outsider image and become an unofficial ambassador for country music. In 1993, his album, "This One's Gonna Hurt," was his first to be certified gold, and in 1994, with the release of "Love and Luck," he became a true country music superstar.

Aaron Tippin

⋆ AARON TIPPIN ⋆

MY MOST EMBARRASSING moment happened while giving a concert in Klammoth Falls, Oregon, a couple of years ago. As I was performing, I was informed through my ear monitors that my fly was unzipped.

A flush of red covered my face I'm sure! Come to find out a fan had located my tour manager and told him about the situation and he in turn relayed the message to the sound engineer who relayed the message to me via my ear monitors.

Boy, how embarrassing. I was halfway through the show!

AARON TIPPIN RELEASED his first album in 1991. Titled "You've Got To Stand For Something," it gave him his first No. 1 hit "There Ain't Nothin' Wrong With the Radio," along with several Top 10 hits, including "My Blue Angel," "I Wouldn't Have It Any Other Way" and "Working Man's Ph. D." He followed that up in 1992 with the platinum selling album, "Read Between the Lines," and in 1993 with the equally successful, "Call of the Wild." His first three albums sold in excess of 2.5 million units. In 1994 he released his fourth album for RCA, "Lookin' Back At Myself." His most recent album is "Tool Box," released in late 1995.

A former truck driver and mechanic, Aaron has turned his blue-collar background into an important element of his music and carved an identifiable niche for himself in a field that is becoming increasingly competitive for male recording artists. He sometimes shows up at concerts wearing a hard hat, a tool belt and work gloves. Aaron also has received a lot of attention because he is a body builder and has a biscep-buldging physique that sets him apart in an industry that is not known for its devotion to physical fitness.

Aaron is a prolific songwriter. In addition to the songs he has written for himself, he has written songs for other artists, including Charley Pride, Mark Collie and David Ball. He wrote all the songs but one on "Lookin' Back At Myself." "It took me a long time to write those songs because I don't write anything I don't feel," he says. "I try to put together albums that everybody will love. If I'm not interested in doing that, I should just sit on the porch and play to the yard."

Aaron recently purchased a 300-acre farm about 60 miles east of Nashville. Using earth-moving equipment, he cleared the land himself and built his own house, a 2800-square foot log "cabin" that he lives in with his wife, Thea.

Shania Twain

★ SHANIA TWAIN ★

SEVEN OR EIGHT years ago, I was performing in a music club in Canada. As it happened, it was Halloween night and the place was packed. The crowd was having a ton of fun dancing and partying in their costumes.

Out of the blue, or perhaps I should say green, a huge man, suitably dressed as the Incredible Hulk, jumped up onto the stage and picked me up. He hoisted me over his shoulders and walked back down to the dance floor. I really thought that he'd simply sit me back on the stage and join his pals on the dance floor ... but, oh, no! He continued whirling me around the club until I thought I was a true goner.

I didn't know if I was scared or embarrassed, but when the Incredible Hulk finally put me down, the show went on and we all laughed about it afterward.

EVERY YEAR SOMEONE breaks from the country music pack to become an "overnight success." Shania Twain was that person in 1995. When her self-titled debut album was released by Mercury Records in 1993, it was praised by critics but largely ignored by radio and consumers, although one of the singles, "Dance With the One That Brought You," charted in the mid-40s.

While Shania was regrouping musically for her second album, she met record producer Mutt Lange, best known for his work with Foreigner, the Cars and AC/DC. They fell in love and were married in 1994. She asked her new husband to produce her next album, and they decided to write all the songs themselves. The result of that collaboration was "The Woman in Me," released early in 1995. The first single, "Whose Bed Have Your Boots Been Under," was a smash hit, pushing the album into the Top 10 and earning it a double platinum certification by the end of 1995.

"The Woman in Me" was a bold departure from traditional country fare in 1995 and critics loved its crisp production values and high energy vocals. Shania was quick to credit Mutt—"the producer of my dreams and the love of my life"—for his input into the album, but she made it clear that she had a headstart on the project before they met. "Most of the songs are based on what I had been doing for two years before I met him," she told me shortly after the release of the album. "But I would hear him playing guitar around the house, doing a groove, working on a hook, and I would say, 'I have a cool title for that,' and we would go from there."

A native of Canada, Shania is the daughter of a Ojibway Indian father and an Irish mother. She grew up in a wilderness area 500 miles north of Toronto, Ontario. It was while working as a forester in the bush that she began her music career. With the help and encouragement of her parents, who unfortunately were killed in an automobile accident in 1986 and never lived to share her success with her, she built a reputation as a top performer in resort areas around Toronto. It was there that she first attracted the attention of Nashville record executives.

Remarkably photogenic, she attracted the attention of Hollywood director John Derek, who photographed her on his California ranch and, with the help of his wife, actress Bo Derek, produced the first two videos for "The Woman in Me." The photographs appeared on the album sleeve and in a calendar Shania's record label distributed as a promotional tool.

Leroy Van Dyke

★ LEROY VAN DYKE ★

WE HAD A show on a Saturday afternoon at O'Keefe Center in Toronto. Ontario, with the Stoneman Family, Boots Randolph and Eddy Arnold. Using a combination of air and ground transportation, we were able to make it to the Coldwater, Michigan, fair for a show that same night.

Upon arrival at the grounds, just a few minutes ahead of show time, we found that there were no facilities, and I had not been to the bathroom for hours. There was no shelter, cover or restroom within two hundred yards, and it was almost show time.

I stood close to the back of the stage, relieved myself, then as an afterthought, leaned over and looked under the stage in the direction of the audience. Looking back at me were three sets of eyes belonging to three girls sitting on the front row. There was no skirting on the front of the stage!

FROM 1957 TO 1977 Leroy Van Dyke scored with 19 hits on *Billboard's* country chart, but no one has ever had a bigger hit than "Walk On By," a song Van Dyke recorded in 1961 for Mercury Records. The record debuted on the chart in September. Within four weeks it went to No. 1 and stayed there for an incredible 37 weeks. Billboard took note of the song in 1995 in its 100th anniversary issue when it declared "Walk On By" the "No. 1 Country Single of All Time." Only five other records have spent more time at No. 1 than "Walk On By" and they were all released before 1958. The song also went to No. 5 on the pop chart, making it the first major country crossover hit and earning Van Dyke a Grammy nomination.

But "Walk On By" was not Van Dyke's first hit. In 1956 he had a Top 10 country hit with "Auctioneer." As a result of the success of that song, he was given a starring role in the movie, "What Am I Bid?"

In a career that spans four decades, Van Dyke has recorded more than 500 songs and released 36 albums. Although he is no longer a major force on radio, he stills performs more than 100 concerts annually, logging an estimated 100,000 road miles a year.

Van Dyke lives in Smithton, Missouri, with his son, Ben, on a 860-acre farm on which he cross-breeds Arabian horses with mules. A licensed auctioneer, he frequently hosts major auctions around the country when he is not doing concert dates.

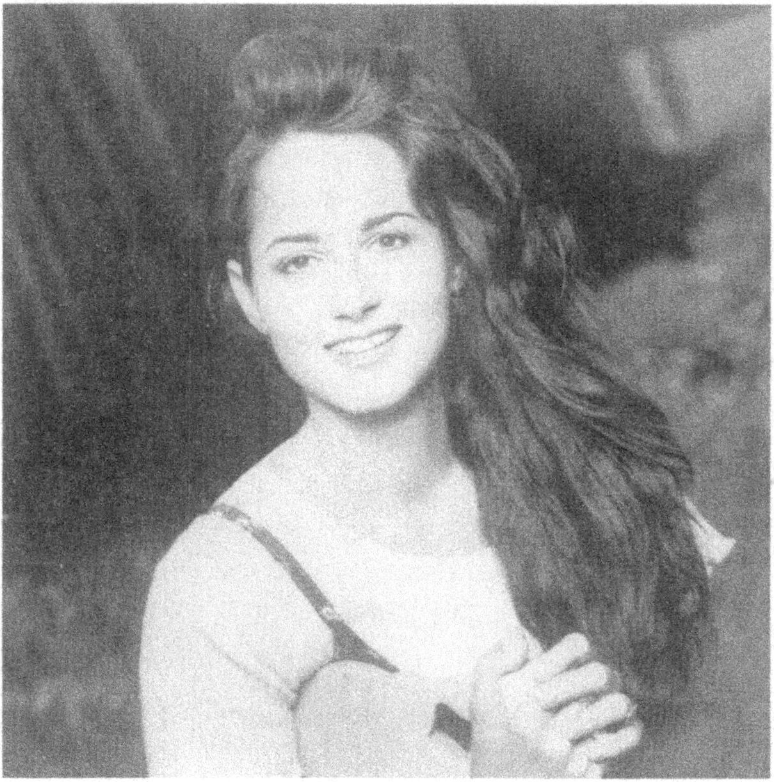

Photo by Ron Keith

Chely Wright

★ CHELY WRIGHT ★

AFTER I MOVED to Nashville I worked at Opryland for four seasons. It has an outdoor theater and the crowd sits right down in front of the stage. There was this thing we called the moat that we had to jump over to get to other parts of the stage. At the bottom of the moat were rocks and sharp objects. Since we didn't want to fall into the moat, we had to jump very high to clear it.

We were doing this dance—it was very choreographed, and everyone on stage was doing the same dance—where we were supposed to run from the top part of the stage and jump five or six feet in the air over the moat and then land on a ramp in front of the crowd.

Well, I jumped and kicked my feet up like I was supposed to do, but I had on a short skirt and my heel got caught in the hem of my skirt. I skidded, face first, about three or four rows into the crowd with my dress up over my head. Lucky for me, this family from Kentucky caught me.

I fractured my kneecap, and I was bleeding, but I was so embarrassed I got up and finished the dance anyway. So I had blood all over, tears coming out of my eyes, ripped panty hose and no pride whatsoever.

CHELY WRIGHT TURNED the music industry on its ear in 1995 when she took home an important award from the Academy of Country Music — Top New Female Vocalist. The previous year she had released her debut album, "Woman in the Moon," to rave reviews by critics who liked her traditional approach to country music.

For Wright, the fastest way to advance has been to look back while moving forward. Tradition, and those who helped shape it, are important to her. It shows in the songs she writes and in the songs she selects. After legendary songwriter Harlan Howard penned her debut single, "He's A Good Ole Boy," the two became good friends.

"He can write a female country song because he takes the time to stay in touch with how people feel, and he's still excited about writing songs," says Wright. "He said, 'I'm so proud of this record. I'm so proud that you're carrying the flag for country music.' If nothing ever happens with my career, if this is as far as I go, just to have Harlan give me a hug and thank me for recording his song, that's about it for me!"

After gaining experience as a performer in the Ozarks while in high school, Chely began her professional career as a singer at Opryland USA, where she worked for five seasons before attracting the attention of music executives at Polydor Records in Nashville. At 23, she found a record label—and a vehicle for a lifelong dream.

"I've never had a memory in my life that didn't include this dream," she says. "Not one time did my parents ever say, 'No, that's not a good idea.' I said, 'I'm gonna be a country music star,' and they said, "We know it.' They did everything they could to help me. My career was a family project."

INDEX

ABOUT THE AUTHOR

JAMES DICKERSON HAS written about celebrities for more than 20 years. The author of *Coming Home: 21 Conversations About Memphis Music*, and *Goin' Back to Memphis: A Century of Blues, Rock'n'Roll and Glorious Soul*, he is the former editor/publisher of *Nine-O-One Network*, a bimonthly publication that was one of the largest circulation music magazines in the country at the time it suspended publication in 1989. He was the executive producer of a nationally syndicated radio program, "Pulsebeat — Voice of the Heartland."

Dickerson has worked as a staff writer for a number of newspapers, including the *Jackson Daily News*, the Greenwood *Commonwealth*, the *Delta Democrat-Times* and *The Commercial Appeal*. The author of over 1400 published articles, columns, poems and short stories, he is one of the most prolific writers in the South today. He recently finished a biography of guitar legend Scotty Moore, titled *That's Alright, Elvis*, and he is currently working on a history of the civil rights movement in Mississippi and Memphis, *Dixie's Dirty Secret: An Un-American Tragedy*.

ISBN 1-888952-33-4

9 781888 952339